TABLE OF CONTENTS

DINOSAURS

The world of dinosaurs

Dinosaurs appeared on Earth 230 million years ago at a time when the planet was populated with reptiles, insects and the ancestors of today's mammals. With their impressive size and, in some cases, ferociousness, these incredible creatures reigned over all the other species. Several million years later, but still well before the appearance of human beings, they suddenly disappeared. Paleontologists—scientists who study fossils—have found the remains of many dinosaurs buried in the ground and have identified over 700 species so far. In this chapter, you will learn about a few of the most fascinating ones.

Fossilization

After they died, some dinosaurs were quickly buried under layers of sediment.

The bones then hardened into rock in a process known as fossilization.

Over time, the fossilized bones were uncovered by the rain and wind.

Tyrannosaurus rex

The name Tyrannosaurus rex means "king of the tyrant lizards." This large dinosaur had a highly developed sense of smell. Its powerful jaws could open extremely wide, and its massive head was supported by its thick neck. Its huge, muscular tail helped to keep it balanced. It had approximately 50 teeth, which could tear through the tough skin of its prey and even crush their bones.

Size: 20 feet

Giganotosaurus

This gigantic predator was longer than Tyrannosaurus rex. Its head alone was as long as an adult-sized bicycle. Its two arms were used to grab on to its prey while it devoured its meal.

This giant Tyrannosaurus rex footprint is about 70 million years old.

Size: 18 feet

The word "dinosaur" means "terrible lizard."

LARGE HERBIVORES

Iguanodon

Iguanodon lived in herds, similar to today's cows. Its beak-shaped snout was used to munch on leaves. Its hands featured four long fingers. It walked on four legs but could stand up on its back legs.

Size: 16 feet

Instead of a thumb, it had a very long spike.

Its nostrils were located on top of its snout.

Diplodocus

This giant had a long, tapered tail that it could flick like a whip.

Brachiosaurus

This giant herbivore spent most of its time eating. It had a tiny head and brain, and a very long neck made up of 12 massive vertebrae. Like a giraffe, its back legs were shorter than its front legs.

Size: 40 feet

SMALL CARNIVORES

Coelophysis

Several Coelophysis fossils have been discovered buried together in the same place, which suggests that they may have hunted in a pack. This dinosaur got around on its hind legs and could run very fast. It had extremely sharp vision. Its bones were hollow, like a bird's.

Size: 4 feet

Oviraptor

Oviraptor means "egg thief," but this dinosaur didn't actually steal eggs. Instead, it incubated them like a chicken.

Carnivores are animals that eat meat. Herbivores eat plants, among other things.

Size: 4 feet

Velociraptor

This compact hunter took down its prey with its back legs and then tore apart its victim's flesh with its razor-sharp teeth. Even though it couldn't fly, Velociraptor was covered in feathers. Its stiff tail helped it change directions quickly, and it had a curved claw on each back foot. Velociraptor was a very fast runner.

BONE-HEADED DINOSAURS

Parasaurolophus

Parasaurolophus may have used its enormous crest to produce sounds, like an elephant. It had a long snout shaped like a duckbill, and its tail was quite stiff. It foraged for food on all fours but ran on its hind legs.

up to 6 feet

Size: 13 feet

Pachycephalosaurus

These dinosaurs sometimes faced off in violent battles. Its name means "thick-headed lizard." Its back legs helped propel it forward when attacking an opponent. Its bony skull protected its brain like a helmet, and its wide eyes suggest that it had excellent vision.

Scientists have found fossilized imprints of dinosaur skin. However, it's impossible to know what color the animals were.

Size: 6.5 feet

HORNED DINOSAURS

Paleontologists believe Triceratops used its large frill to impress or attract a mate, like a peacock when it fans out its tail.

Triceratops

Triceratops charged other dinosaurs when it felt threatened. Each of its toes was tipped with a hoof-shaped nail. It had three horns: two big ones above its eyes and a smaller one on its snout.

Its beak was hooked like an eagle's and it had no teeth.

Size: 13 feet

Styracosaurus

Although much smaller than Triceratops, Styracosaurus was still quite imposing. Its bony frill was adorned with long horns, and its legs were short and muscular.

Size: 6.5 feet

Fossilized dinosaur excrement has revealed all sorts of information about these creatures.

ARMORED DINOSAURS

Edmontonia

A quadruped and an herbivore, Edmontonia was one of the last dinosaurs to have roamed the Earth. It used its spiked tail to defend itself and its sturdy legs to stay balanced during combat. Its body was covered in protective armor from nose to tail. Its narrow snout was used to forage for plants on the ground.

Size: 10 feet

The largest fossilized dinosaur egg ever found measured 20 inches and weighed 20 pounds, which is 170-times the weight of a chicken egg.

Euoplocephalus

This dinosaur probably lived in herds and was capable of defending itself against large predators. Its core was mostly immobile underneath its bony armor, but its front legs were very agile. The bony growth at the end of its tail was used like a club, and it could trip other dinosaurs by swiping at their legs.

Size: 8 feet

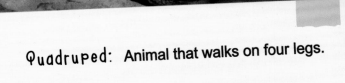

Quadruped: Animal that walks on four legs.

8

PLATED AND SAILBACKED DINOSAURS

Stegosaurus

Scientists believe that its armor could change colors. Its head was small compared to the rest of its body, and it had a tiny brain. Its tail was tipped with several long spikes used to defend against predators. The bony plates on its back were shaped like arrowheads.

Size: 14 feet

Spinosaurus

It resembled Ouranosaurus and would have lived during the same period, but Spinosaurus was a carnivore.

What's the same size as a dinosaur but weighs nothing?

A dinosaur's shadow

Ouranosaurus

This herbivore had a large sail on its back that allowed it to regulate its body temperature. Its neck was quite flexible, and it could stand on its hind legs.

Size: 10 feet

IN THE AIR...

Archaeopteryx

The ancestor of modern birds, Archaeopteryx was roughly the size of a pigeon. According to the latest discoveries, this dinosaur could fly short distances, like a pheasant. Its body was covered with soft down or feathers, and its long back legs were used to catch its prey. It had a very long, bony tail.

Quetzalcoatlus

Quetzalcoatlus was the size of a small airplane and had a 40-foot wingspan. Its beak was very long and sharp.

Pterodactyl

Pterodactyl was a winged reptile capable of gliding. Its wings consisted of a thin membrane of skin, much like a bat's.

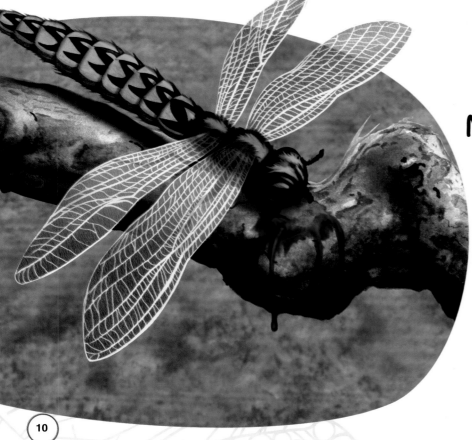

Meganeura

Meganeura was a prehistoric meat-eating dragonfly. Without a doubt, it was the largest flying insect to ever exist on Earth!

Even before the dinosaurs appeared, Earth was teeming with another lifeform: insects and other arthropods. Cockroaches, spiders, snails and scorpions have been evolving on our planet for millions of years.

... AND UNDER THE SEA

Kronosaurus

Kronosaurus is a member of the plesiosaur family. This marine predator was the most fearsome to have ever swum the seas. Its jaw was lined with cone-shaped teeth, and its four fins made it a very fast swimmer.

Ichthyosaurus

Like other marine reptiles, it evolved from land reptiles. Ichthyosaurus needed to come up to the surface of the water for air. Its fins helped it change directions quickly, and it propelled itself through the water by moving its body from side to side, like a shark.

Archelon

This ancient turtle, the biggest that ever existed, lived in the prehistoric oceans. Its beak was powerful enough to crush hard-shelled crustaceans and mollusks and dig for food on the seafloor. Its shell was made up of a leathery membrane.

Species of bony fish became more diversified during the Triassic period, 250 million years ago.

Triassic period: A geologic period in Earth's history that took place between 252 and 201 million years ago.

THE END OF A DYNASTY

The dinosaurs were wiped out 65 million years ago. Scientists have several clues that would explain this massive extinction.

United States

Mexico

The Chicxulub crater

In the 1980s, traces were found of the place where a giant asteroid collided with the Earth. The force of the impact left behind an enormous crater.

The asteroid measured some 6 miles in diameter and struck with a force 1,000,000-times more powerful than an atomic bomb! The atmospheric effects of the impact caused much of Earth's plant life to disappear and eventually led to the extinction of the dinosaurs.

Asteroid: Chunk of metal and rock from outer space.

PALEONTOLOGY

It takes paleontologists a lot of time and patience to unearth dinosaur bones. They use a hammer and chisel to remove the top layers of rock, then more precision tools to clear away the dust from around the bones.

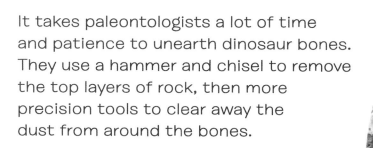

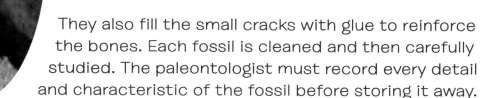

They also fill the small cracks with glue to reinforce the bones. Each fossil is cleaned and then carefully studied. The paleontologist must record every detail and characteristic of the fossil before storing it away.

The fossils we see in museums are put together like giant jigsaw puzzles. Most of the time, replicas made from resin, which is much lighter than rock, are used to make the animal look as lifelike as possible—a daunting task that the paleontologist often works with an artist to accomplish.

FARM ANIMALS

Once upon a time, there was a farm

Agriculture and breeding practices emerged some 12,000 years ago, when the first farmers identified the tamest and hardiest animals for their purposes. Over the centuries, new breeds were created that were perfectly adapted to their climate and their "workload."

Barns

To protect them against wild animals and thieves, farm animals are kept in enclosures located near the main house so the farmer can keep a close eye on them. Barns help shelter the animals from storms, cold snaps or heatwaves.

The older I get, the stinkier I am. What am I?

Cheese!

Pantry staples

Farm animals are a source of meat, milk, fat and eggs, as well as feathers, wool and leather, which are used to make a wide variety of items, including cheese, oil, clothing, blankets, bags and shoes.

Shepherd

Animals raised for meat are kept in a pasture where they graze on fresh grass. The shepherd watches over his herd day and night. In some parts of the world, shepherds practice transhumance, leading their herd into the mountains for the summer.

Sheepdog

This breed of dog has a natural herding instinct, running circles around sheep scattered across a meadow to drive them back together. It can also make the herd advance by running behind it from side to side.

Wolf: ancestor of the dog

It's long been said that the dog is man's best friend! More than 20,000 years ago, prehistoric humans domesticated a pack of wolves, keeping and breeding the tamest among them. Since then, 344 breeds of dog have been developed for their specific temperaments and talents.

Enclosure: Plot of land surrounded by a fence.

Heatwave: Period of intense heat that can cause dehydration.

Transhumance: Seasonal movement of animals to new pastures.

BOVINES

Domestic cow

The cow is a ruminant that spends more than eight hours a day digesting its food. It grazes on grass, which it grinds with its teeth. Food is regurgitated from its rumen back into its mouth, where it is mixed with saliva and chewed for a second time. The food then passes through the three other parts of the cow's stomach, where it is digested.

Yak

Native to the Himalayan mountain range, this bovine is known for its long, thick fur that protects it from the icy temperatures and strong winds that prevail at high altitudes. The Tibetans raise yaks for their milk, meat, hides and dung, which is used as fuel for cooking and heating.

The bison has a highly developed sense of smell. It can distinguish odors from 2 miles away.

American bison

Among the largest animals in North America, wild bison once roamed the continent's vast grasslands by the millions. Today, most bison can be found on farms. In the spring, the female gives birth to one calf, which she nurses for a full year.

Dairy cow

For a cow to produce milk, it must first give birth to a calf. After that, the farmer milks the cow twice a day, morning and evening. The cow produces milk for 10 months. There are several breeds of dairy cow, including Holstein, Normande and Jersey.

Normande cow

Holstein cow

Jersey cow

What language does the word "yak" come from?

Tibetan

Cheese

Before milk can be made into cheese, it has to be left to curdle, a process during which it separates into small clumps. It is then poured into molds and strained to remove the whey. Salt is added to help the cheese stay fresh longer. Some cheeses are aged for several years, which is what gives them their sharp flavor!

Butter

Butter is made from the cream that separates from the milk. The cream is churned, or beaten, until it turns into butter. The remaining liquid is called buttermilk.

Ruminant: Animal with a 3- or 4-compartment stomach that lets it regurgitate food into its mouth.

Rumen: First compartment of a ruminant's stomach.

EQUINES

Equines are mammals. These herbivores have hooves made up of a single digit.

Workhorse

Known for its strength and stamina, the workhorse is taller and heavier than other breeds of horses. It was used for centuries on farms until it was replaced by the tractor. In developing countries, the workhorse is still used to pull carts and agricultural equipment used to work the land.

Mule

A cross between a male donkey and a female horse, the mule has all the same features as a donkey but is bigger and stronger. The hybridization of these two species makes their offspring infertile. Because of this, the female mule can't have babies.

Donkey

Another equine species, the donkey is a small animal, but very docile, patient and strong. It may be stubborn, but that's because it's very smart and can sense danger! It can turn its long ears 180 degrees independently of each other to tune into surrounding noises.

What do you call a donkey with three legs?

A wonky donkey

18

Mare and foal

A female horse, called a mare, can reproduce starting at three years old. After an 11-month pregnancy, she gives birth to one foal; in rare cases, she will have two babies. Between one and three hours after birth, the foal is already able to stand up and walk on its long, spindly legs.

Miniature horse

The miniature horse is small but, unlike a pony, its body is proportioned more like a horse's. It is often kept as a pet.

Pony

A pony is a small horse with a thick mane, heavy coat and short legs. Well-trained ponies are often ridden by children.

Did you know that a horse's teeth never stop growing?

Herbivore: Animal that eats plants.

Hybridization: Crossbreeding of two different animal or plant species.

WHAT A COAT!

Sheep

Raised for thousands of years, the sheep is popular for its meat, especially lamb. Sheep's wool is used to make clothing, blankets and mattresses. The breeder must shear the sheep's fleece once or twice a year during the summer months.

Alpaca

A member of the camel family, the alpaca is native to South America. It's raised mainly for its wool, although its meat is becoming increasingly popular. Unlike the llama, the alpaca is not a pack animal.

Why does a llama spit? As a way of communicating. It won't spit at a person unless it feels threatened.

Llama

The llama is a social animal that prefers to live in groups, which typically include several females and one male. When it senses danger, it emits ear-piercing shrieks to scare off predators. The llama has a two-layered coat: Its long, bristly hair protects it from the rain and snow, and its soft undercoat keeps it warm.

Cashmere goat

This breed of goat comes from the Kashmir region of India and China. The cashmere goat produces cashmere wool. Pashmina, the finest type of cashmere wool, comes from the goat's neck.

Goat

The goat is a very popular animal because it's small and strong. It will eat anything and keeps fields and meadows neat and tidy. Its milk makes delicious cheese! The meat from a baby goat, called a kid, is highly prized in some countries.

Rabbit

This small animal has been raised since the Middle Ages. Rabbits are very prolific breeders, and females can give birth to anywhere between 4 and 12 kits per litter. This mammal does not have a specific mating season; it reproduces year-round.

Angora rabbit

This breed of rabbit is the result of a genetic mutation, which results in its very long, soft fur. Angora rabbits lose their fur regularly, and the breeder collects it by grooming the animals with a fine-tooth comb.

Fleece: Wool from a sheared sheep.

Genetic mutation: Permanent alteration of a gene.

POULTRY

Chicken

Chicken farms are by far the most common type of farm worldwide and account for 90% of all poultry breeding operations. Chickens are also raised for their eggs, which are an inexpensive source of protein.

Turkey

The turkey is native to North America. It was introduced to Europe in the 16th century and is now found all over the world. In the United States, it is eaten for Thanksgiving, and in Canada, it is the traditional Christmas dinner. It is typically served with cranberries.

What sound does a turkey make?

Gobble gobble!

Goose

The goose is a highly prized animal in China, where goose farms abound. It's raised for its meat, but also for its down and its feathers, which are used to make pillows and duvets.

Duck

The duck is very popular in Asia. They're raised outdoors and congregate in groups. Ducks are highly resistant to disease and don't drink very much water. Its meat is leaner than that of other poultry. Its body and wings are covered with approximately 12,000 feathers, which fall out once a year.

Rooster

The rooster always dominates the hens in a henhouse, watching over them and maintaining order. It also wakes up the other birds early in the morning with its crowing! After being fertilized by the rooster, the hen incubates her eggs, which will each hatch a chick.

Pheasant

The pheasant is easily recognized by its brilliantly colored plumage. Its body looks like a chicken's, but the pheasant has long tail feathers that it fans out like a peacock. Like the rooster, the male has bright caruncles.

Quail

The quail is a small, gray, speckled bird with a highly varied diet that includes insects, larvae, grain and grass. Each year, it can lay up to 300 tiny, spotted eggs, which are the most nutritious of any bird's!

Down: Small, fluffy feathers that cover chicks and the bellies of adult birds.

Caruncle: Red or brightly colored fleshy growth on the head and throat.

FLESH AND FEATHERS

Pig

This highly intelligent animal is raised by farmers around the world. When it comes to "nose to tail" eating, the pig is a prime example, with all parts of the animal being used to make roasts, bacon, ham, sausages, blood sausages and more. A sow can have more than 10 piglets per litter.

Emu

Native to Australia, the emu first appeared millions of years ago. It's raised for its meat and feathers, but also for its oil, which is used in the production of cream and soap.

Ostrich

Like the emu, the ostrich is a flightless bird. But unlike the emu, ostriches have just two toes on each foot tipped with sharp nails. The female lays a giant egg roughly the size of 24 chicken eggs. Breeders hatch the eggs in incubators.

Incubator: Electric-powered enclosure used to keep eggs warm until they hatch.

AROUND THE WORLD

A newborn elephant calf weighs more than 220 pounds!

Elephant

People have been riding atop the Asian elephant for thousands of years. It's also used for heavy lifting in the tropical forests, as a mount for hunting and as a method of transportation. The mahout—the elephant's rider, trainer or keeper—looks after the animal for its entire life, riding it and caring for it.

Silkworm

The caterpillars of the silkmoth (Bombyx mori) are raised to make silk, which is obtained from the cocoons that the insects spin during their life cycle. Silkworm rearing operations also cultivate mulberry trees for their leaves, which the caterpillar feeds on exclusively.

Crocodile

Crocodiles (and alligators) are raised mainly for their meat and their skin, which is worth its weight in gold. Kept in large ponds, the animals are fed a diet of meat scraps and by-products. Crocodile eggs are collected and hatched in incubators.

Reindeer

This cervid species has been raised for thousands of years in the cold climates of northern Europe, where farming is a challenge. Reindeer follow the herders' movements, grazing along the way. They migrate to the pastures in summer and to forested areas in winter.

WILD ANIMALS

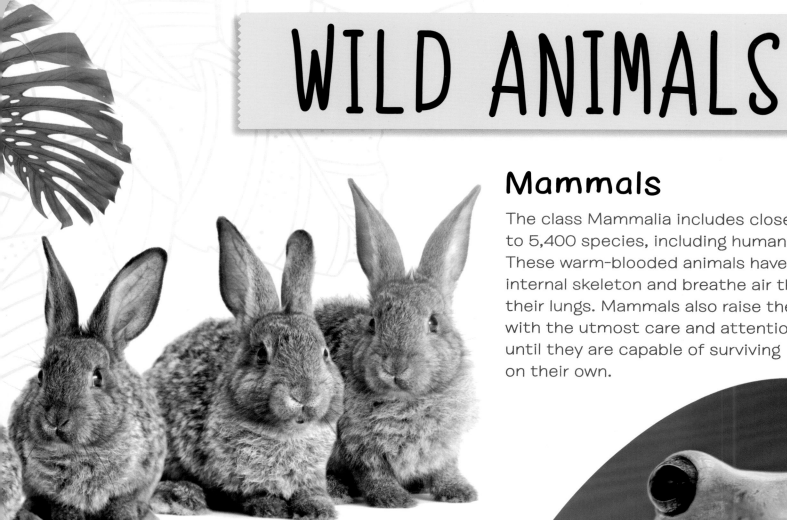

Mammals

The class Mammalia includes close to 5,400 species, including humans. These warm-blooded animals have an internal skeleton and breathe air through their lungs. Mammals also raise their young with the utmost care and attention until they are capable of surviving on their own.

Amphibians

Amphibians lead a semi-aquatic life, reproducing, laying their eggs and developing in the water. Amphibians develop lungs in adulthood to replace the gills they were born with; this allows them to live on land.

Fish

There are more than 30,000 species of fish on the planet, living in the fresh water of rivers, lakes and streams, and in the saltwater of estuaries, seas and oceans. They breathe through their gills and move through the water with their fins. They were the first vertebrates to have populated the Earth.

Gills: Organs that allow an aquatic animal to breathe by extracting oxygen from the water.

Vertebrate: Any animal that has a spine.

Birds

Bird species have two legs and a pair of wings, but that doesn't mean they are all capable of flight. All birds lay eggs, which they incubate in a nest. The chicks are protected and fed by their parents.

Reptiles

This class includes turtles, crocodiles, snakes and lizards. Reptiles' bodies are covered with scales, and their core temperature fluctuates in response to the environment. Reptiles lay eggs with strong, hard shells.

Arthropods

Arthropods account for 80% of all animal species and include insects, crustaceans, spiders and millipedes. All arthropods have an exoskeleton and jointed limbs.

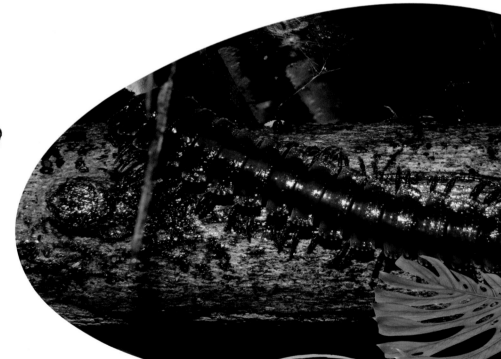

Mollusks

Mollusks have a visible or hidden shell; their body is usually soft and boneless. Oysters, snails and octopuses belong to this class of animals.

There are three final categories of animals: sea stars, which have a skeleton embedded in their skin; worms, which have a body made up of rings; and jellyfish, which have venomous harpoon-like stingers.

ANIMALS OF THE FOREST

Gray wolf

The gray wolf lives and hunts in a group of 6 to 12 individuals. The pack is led by a dominant male and female. This canid's howling can be heard for up to 6 miles in all directions and is a way of signaling the boundaries of the pack's territory.

Class: Mammal
Size: 3-5 feet long
Home: North America, Europe and Asia

What does an owl with an attitude have?

A scowl

Great horned owl

The largest owl in the Americas is easily recognized by its ear tufts, small bunches of feathers that look like two horns. Its vision and smell are extremely sharp, allowing it to hunt small animals, such as mice, frogs and insects, at night.

Class: Bird
Size: 1.5-2 feet tall
Home: North and South America

Moose

The male moose has a pair of antlers that fall off and grow back each year. It feeds on aquatic plants, tree bark, moss and pine cones. This enormous mammal is a very strong swimmer: Its hooves are splayed, and it can even dive underwater for food.

Class: Mammal
Size: 8-10 feet long
Home: North America, Europe and Asia

Wolverine

The wolverine is a small but fierce animal, often attacking prey much bigger than itself. This omnivore lives away from humans, in the evergreen forests of the Northern Hemisphere. Its paws are tipped with powerful claws that it uses to dig, climb and hunt.

Class: Mammal
Size: 2-3 feet long
Home: North America and Europe

Beaver

This rodent builds dams on rivers made out of branches and mud. The entrance to the beaver lodge is underwater to protect the animals from land-bound predators. Beavers slap their flat tails on the surface of the water when they sense danger.

Class: Mammal
Size: 2.5-4 feet long
Home: North America and Europe

Wood frog

During the cold season, the wood frog hibernates above ground or in a bed of leaves. It has a remarkable ability that allows it to survive the winter: It freezes. Come the spring, it thaws out again and resumes its normal routine.

Class: Amphibian / **Size:** 2-3 inches long / **Home:** North America

What's another name for a wolverine?

Skunk bear

Omnivore: Animal that eats both plants and meat.
Pack: Group of wolves or dogs that live together.
Canid: Family of mammals that includes wolves, dogs, foxes and jackals.

ANIMALS OF THE JUNGLE

Jaguar

The jaguar is a carnivore. It stalks its prey silently, because it can only run fast for short distances. It feeds on small mammals, such as the tapir, as well as fish and turtles.

Class: Mammal
Size: 5-6 feet long
Home: Central and South America

Sloth

The sloth is the slowest animal on the planet. In its upside-down position on a branch, it moves at a maximum speed of 2 meters per minute! This herbivore eats tender shoots, buds, leaves and fruit.

Class: Mammal
Size: 1.5-2 feet tall
Home: South America

King cobra

When it feels threatened, the king cobra rises up and flares out its hood, which is patterned with characteristic markings. Its powerful venom can be fatal to humans who are not quickly given the antivenom.

Class: Reptile
Size: 10-18 feet long
Home: Asia

The sloth spends most of its life hanging upside down.

Gorilla

The gorilla is the biggest and strongest of all the primates. While a male gorilla can weigh up to three times as much as a human, the female of the species is much smaller. These animals live in troops consisting of 3 to 30 individuals, led by a dominant silverback, an adult male recognizable by its silver fur.

Class: Mammal
Size: 4.5-6 feet tall
Home: Africa

Koko was a gorilla who learned to speak sign language. She had a vocabulary of more than 1,000 words!

Tiger

The tiger's characteristic stripes help keep it camouflaged so it can sneak up on its prey. It prefers to live in the dense forest, which is better suited to its hunting techniques. The tiger is also one of the strongest swimmers in the feline family.

Class: Mammal
Size: 5-9 feet long
Home: Asia

Keel-billed toucan

This bird is known for its large, multicolored bill that can measure up to half the length of its body. The keel-billed toucan uses this very light, banana-shaped appendage to reach for fruit, which makes up most of its diet.

Class: Bird / **Size:** 1.5-2 feet long / **Home:** South America

Carnivore: Animal that eats meat.
Herbivore: Animal that eats plants.
Primate: Order of mammals that includes lemurs, monkeys and humans.

ANIMALS OF THE SAVANNAH

Lion

Males and females have clearly defined roles within a pride of lions. The females hunt in a group, while the males roar and protect their territory. Despite their fearsome appearance, male lions are very lazy, sleeping for up to 20 hours a day.

Class: Mammal
Size: Up to 5 feet long
Home: Africa, Asia

Giraffe

The giraffe's long neck allows it to reach leaves and fruit growing high in the treetops. On the open savannah, its impressive height also lets it spot predators from very far off. If a giraffe feels threatened, it will take off at a gallop, reaching speeds of 30 miles per hour.

Class: Mammal
Size: Up to 18 feet tall
Home: Africa

Elephant

The elephant uses its trunk to suck up liquids and to grasp food and other objects. Its boneless trunk is actually made up of thousands of small muscles and is an extension of its upper lip and nose, combined into one appendage.

Class: Mammal / **Size:** Up to 13 feet tall / **Home:** Africa, Asia

Did you know that a giraffe's tongue is so long that it can lick its own ears?

Ostrich

Since the ostrich is too heavy to fly, it needs to run very fast in order to survive. Its top speed is 43 miles per hour. Ostrich chicks are born knowing how to run.

Class: Bird
Size: Up to 9 feet tall
Home: Africa

Meerkat

The meerkat isn't nicknamed the "sentinel of the desert" for nothing! Meerkats stand on their hind legs to keep watch or to scan for food. They live in colonies of several individuals and communicate with each other by barking or whistling.

Class: Mammal
Size: 10-12 inches tall
Home: Africa

Rhinoceros

The rhinoceros has poor eyesight. It suffers from nearsightedness, or myopia, and can't see beyond 100 feet in front of it. When it feels threatened, this usually peaceful herbivore is known to charge, horn first, straight at the source of the danger.

Class: Mammal
Size: 11-14 feet long
Home: Africa

Myopia: Vision condition in which objects farther away appear blurry.

ANIMALS OF THE DESERT

Kangaroo

At birth, the baby kangaroo, or joey, measures only a few inches long. It is blind and completely defenseless. It clings onto its mother's fur and slowly pulls itself into the pouch on her belly, where it can nurse and finish growing. It stays there for several months until it's able to move around independently.

Class: Mammal
Size: 3-8 feet tall
Home: Oceania

Scorpion

The scorpion has a long tail that curls forward over its back, distinguishing it from other arachnids. It has a venomous stinger and two pincers that it uses to grab and crush its prey. This nocturnal predator feeds mainly on insects and spiders.

Class: Arthropod
Size: Up to 7 inches long
Home: Africa, North America, South America, Asia, Oceania

Did you know that a kick from a kangaroo can kill a human?

Fennec fox

The fennec fox is easily recognized by its long, pointed ears, which it uses to pinpoint its prey. Native to the Sahara Desert, this fox is the smallest canid in the world. The soles of its paws are covered with fur to provide traction when chasing its prey over the sand. It feeds on lizards, birds, insects and small mammals. It can burrow as deep as two meters underground to shelter from the scorching desert heat.

Class: Mammal
Size: 8-16 inches tall
Home: North Africa and the Arabian Peninsula

Desert tortoise

The desert tortoise uses its front legs to dig burrows, where it takes refuge from the extreme desert temperatures. It hibernates underground in its tunnel from October to February.

Class: Reptile
Size: 10-15 inches long
Home: North America

Dromedary

The dromedary is perfectly adapted to life in the desert. Its hump, made of stored fat, allows it to survive for several days without drinking or eating. Its eyes are ringed with long lashes to protect them from the sand, and its nostrils can close during a sandstorm.

Class: Mammal
Size: 7-11 feet tall
Home: Africa, Asia and Australia

Addax

The addax is an extremely rare herbivore that lives in certain parts of the Sahara Desert. Hunting and the destruction of its natural habitat have led to a decline in the population of this small antelope, which is now listed as critically endangered.

Class: Mammal
Size: 5-5.5 feet tall
Home: Africa

Arachnid: Class of arthropods that includes spiders, scorpions and mites.

Sahara Desert: Desert region in North Africa that spans more than 10 countries.

ANIMALS OF THE POLAR REGIONS

Polar bear

An excellent swimmer, the polar bear is right at home in the icy waters of the Arctic. It uses its webbed paws like flippers to swim underwater. It hunts seals on the sea ice, sometimes using deception and sometimes sheer speed to capture its prey.

Class: Mammal
Size: 5-10 feet tall
Home: North America, Asia, Greenland

What animal has black skin and white fur?

The polar bear

Walrus

While the walrus is quite clumsy and awkward on land, it's surprisingly agile in the water. It uses its whiskers to detect food sources on the ocean floor. It then stirs up the sand to uncover the mollusks that make up its diet.

Class: Mammal
Size: 9-12 feet long
Home: North America, Asia, Greenland

Emperor penguin

The largest of all penguin species, the emperor penguin is known to nest more than 100 km from the ocean. After laying a single egg, the female returns to the water in search of food. The male incubates the egg for several weeks until his partner returns.

Class: Bird / **Size:** Up to 4 feet tall / **Home:** Antarctic

Snowy owl

This large bird of prey is an all-around skilled hunter. With its unmatched eyesight and hearing, the snowy owl can track its prey at great distances. This raptor feeds on lemmings, rabbits, hares and other small mammals.

Class: Bird
Size: 20-28 inches long
Home: North America, Asia, Greenland

Arctic fox

This small carnivore, a cousin to the red fox, lives in the plains, mountains and tundras of the Northern Hemisphere. The arctic fox's fur turns brown in the summer and fall, and back to white when winter returns.

Class: Mammal
Size: 16-27 inches long
Home: North America, Asia, Europe, Greenland

Muskox

The muskox's two layers of fur protect this gentle herbivore against the cold and snow. Because food is scarce during the winter, the muskox is forced to move very slowly to conserve its energy.

Class: Mammal / **Size:** 4-5 feet tall
Home: North America

Northern Hemisphere: Part of the planet that is north of the equator.

INSECTS AND OTHER CRITTERS

They crawl, swim, walk and fly... These little creatures are so well adapted to life on Earth that they make up 80% of all known animal species. They're members of the arthropod family, and they're invertebrates, which means they have no spine. Instead, they have an exoskeleton—a skeleton on the outside of their body.

Time to find out more about the three main groups in the arthropod family!

Insects

There are more than one million species of insects living on the planet. Three out of every four animals on Earth are insects. According to entomologists, there could be millions of others still out there waiting to be discovered! Insects have six legs and can have two or four wings, although some insects are wingless. Their body is made up of three parts: the head, the thorax and the abdomen. They have compound eyes.

Arachnids

Arachnids have eight legs. They don't have wings or antennae and have simple eyes. This group includes spiders and scorpions.

Myriapods

Myriapods, known as millipedes, have anywhere from 18 to 750 legs. They also have two antennae, mandibles, and one or two pairs of maxillae.

MASTERS OF DISGUISE

Some species of predatory insects have perfected the art of camouflage. This ability is also an important defense mechanism for insects, because it helps them blend in with their surroundings.

The owl butterfly's wings feature black eyespots ringed with yellow that resemble owl or frog eyes.

This caterpillar is the same shape and color as a branch, making it hard for predators to spot.

What is a caterpillar?

A worm wearing a fur coat!

The praying mantis sits and waits patiently for its prey to approach.

At rest with its wings closed, this orange oakleaf butterfly looks like a dead leaf.

FLYING INSECTS

Butterflies

Butterflies are some of the most colorful and admired insects on Earth. More than 200,000 species of these winged insects exist. They come in all sizes and colors and are divided into two families: diurnal butterflies and nocturnal butterflies.

Butterflies go through several transformations before reaching adulthood. This life cycle is known as "metamorphosis."

The female butterfly lays her eggs (1) on a leaf. Tiny caterpillars soon emerge. These butterfly larvae will molt several times during their life cycle.

The caterpillar (2) spins a cocoon (3), in which it turns into a chrysalis (4). The caterpillar's body undergoes a complete metamorphosis. After a few weeks, a butterfly emerges from the chrysalis.

If you look at a butterfly's wing under a microscope, you'll see that it's made up of thousands of tiny scales. A butterfly's wings are very fragile and easily damaged, which is why you should never touch them.

Diurnal butterflies: Butterflies that are active during the day.

Nocturnal butterflies: Butterflies that are active at night. They are less colorful and have thicker hair.

Molt: To shed the exoskeleton when it becomes too small.

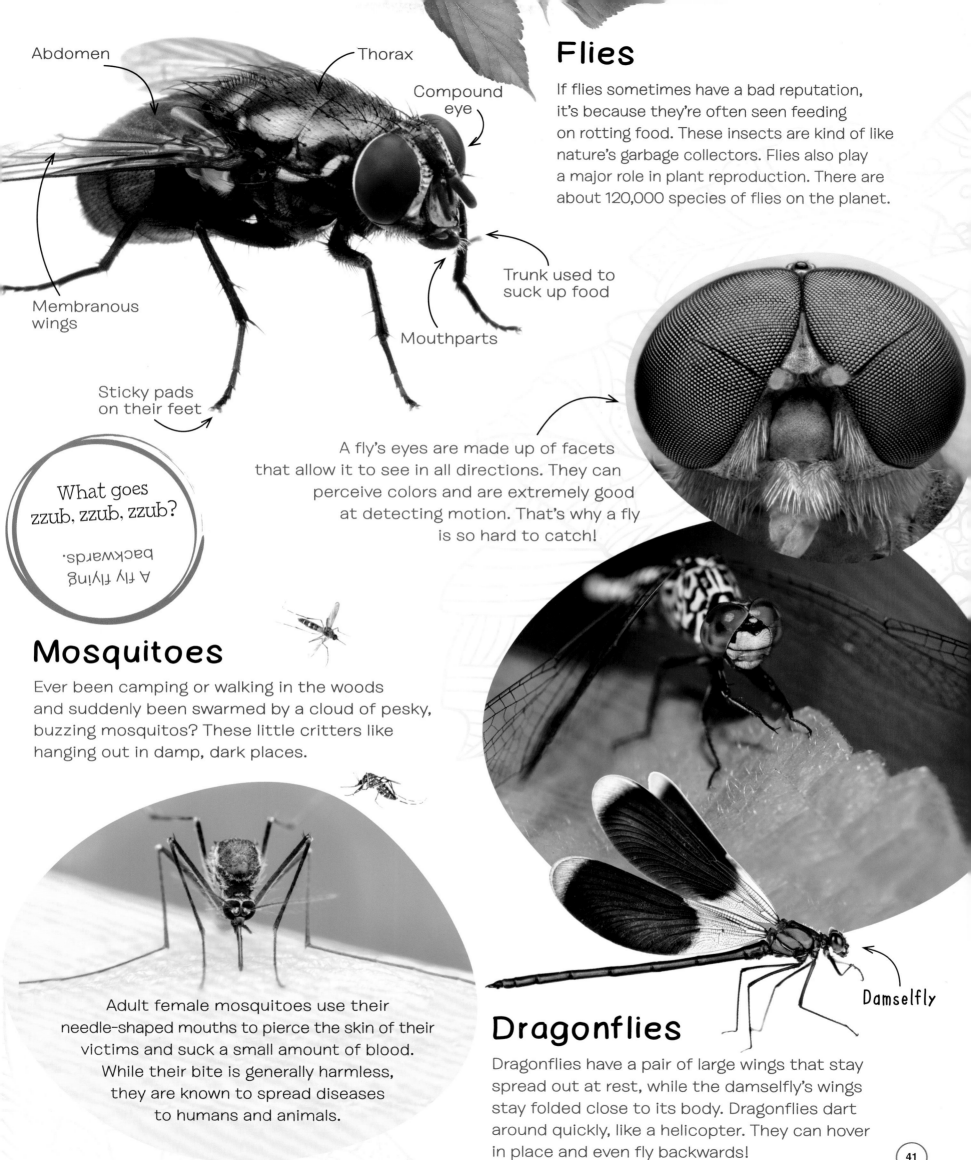

Abdomen

Thorax

Compound eye

Flies

If flies sometimes have a bad reputation, it's because they're often seen feeding on rotting food. These insects are kind of like nature's garbage collectors. Flies also play a major role in plant reproduction. There are about 120,000 species of flies on the planet.

Trunk used to suck up food

Membranous wings

Mouthparts

Sticky pads on their feet

What goes zzub, zzub, zzub?

A fly flying backwards.

A fly's eyes are made up of facets that allow it to see in all directions. They can perceive colors and are extremely good at detecting motion. That's why a fly is so hard to catch!

Mosquitoes

Ever been camping or walking in the woods and suddenly been swarmed by a cloud of pesky, buzzing mosquitos? These little critters like hanging out in damp, dark places.

Adult female mosquitoes use their needle-shaped mouths to pierce the skin of their victims and suck a small amount of blood. While their bite is generally harmless, they are known to spread diseases to humans and animals.

Damselfly

Dragonflies

Dragonflies have a pair of large wings that stay spread out at rest, while the damselfly's wings stay folded close to its body. Dragonflies dart around quickly, like a helicopter. They can hover in place and even fly backwards!

SOCIAL INSECTS

Bees

Bees play a vital role in preserving nature's balance. As they travel from flower to flower, they are contributing to pollination, the process necessary for plants to reproduce.

Worker

The workers are all female. Their jobs include building the wax cells, depositing the honey, feeding the larvae, producing the royal jelly, and cleaning the hive. Each worker has her own specific task!

Queen

Inside the hive

A bee colony is made up of a single queen, tens of thousands of workers, and drones.

Twice the size of a worker bee, the queen is the only female in the hive capable of reproducing: She can lay up to 1,500 eggs per day. These are deposited in honeycomb cells and soon hatch into larvae, which in turn grow into new bees.

The foraging worker bees travel from flower to flower collecting nectar and pollen. They typically stay within a 3-mile radius of the hive.

Drone

The drones are all male. Their job is to try to reproduce with the queen. When it's time for the queen to lay her eggs, they are kicked out of the hive.

To avoid being stung, the beekeeper wears a special hat equipped with protective netting and blows smoke into the hive to calm the bees.

Pollination: Method of reproduction for certain plants.

Beekeeper: Person who raises bees for their by-products.

Ants

Several thousand species of ants exist. Some are tiny and others can be as long as your little finger. Experts at teamwork, ants live together in organized colonies.

To communicate with each other, ants rub antennae and emit sounds and substances called pheromones.

Their eyes can detect motion, but they can't see objects up close.

The sensors on their antennae allow them to smell, touch and taste.

Food is digested in their abdomen.

Their mandibles are used to carry or tear apart objects and to dig underground tunnels and chambers.

Their thorax houses their heart and the powerful muscles that control their legs.

Ants can lift several times their own body weight. They sometimes work together to carry bigger objects.

Termites

Like ants, termites live in a colony. Termite mounds, made of a mixture of saliva, earth and wood, can reach gigantic sizes. The largest termite mounds ever discovered measured 16 feet high.

JUMPING INSECTS

Fleas and ticks

The cat flea is the most common of all fleas. Despite its name, it also attacks dogs and humans. It can jump more than 100 times its height. For an adult human, that would be the same as jumping 650 feet—the height of a skyscraper!

Fleas don't have wings, but they use their bristly back legs to propel themselves forward. They can jump up to 600 times in an hour, until they find a suitable host.

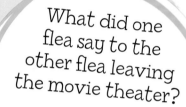

What did one flea say to the other flea leaving the movie theater?

Are we walking home or taking a dog?

Smaller green leafhopper

The smaller green leafhopper is a pretty turquoise-green color. It not only jumps, but it's also a skilled flier. The larvae of this biting-sucking insect feed on plant sap. The leafhopper is capable of wreaking havoc on farmers' fields.

Locusts

These jumping insects lead relatively solitary lives, but weather conditions can sometimes cause swarms of billions of locusts to form. In high winds, a swarm can travel up to 125 miles in a single day!

SINGING INSECTS

Orthoptera belong to more than 20,000 species and come in a variety of shapes and colors. They are found all over the world, except in the polar regions.

Grasshoppers

Grasshoppers use their wings and powerful back legs to get around. Like locusts, crickets and cicadas, they produce high-pitched sounds, all of which are different!

The great green bush-cricket lives in bushes and trees and feeds on tiny bugs, such as slugs, larvae and flies.

Cicadas

The cicadas' distinctive sounds are synonymous with summertime. Male cicadas have special organs called tymbals. A muscle activates the tymbals quickly and repeatedly to produce a high-pitched sound called a stridulation.

Crickets

When it comes time to mate, male crickets produce a distinctive sound by rubbing their wings together. This sound helps them to attract a partner.

In Africa, desert locusts can sometimes form enormous swarms made up of billions of individuals. These clouds of insects can destroy entire crops in no time.

PREDATORY INSECTS

Praying mantises

Perched on their four back legs with their front legs folded, praying mantises wait patiently for their prey. Each species is perfectly camouflaged to look like a flower, a leaf or a branch.

Their big, bulging eyes give them a very wide field of vision.

The praying mantis's body is perfectly designed for hunting. Their flexible neck lets them swivel their head to look over their shoulders.

They use their spiky front legs to hold onto their prey.

Their long back legs are powerfully muscled.

Males and females of the same species are often different sizes and colors. In general, the females are much larger than the males. In some species, the female even devours her partner after mating.

True to their name, spider wasps hunt spiders. These black wasps use their sting to paralyze their prey before dragging it to their burrow. An egg is then laid on the victim, which is eaten alive by the newly hatched larvae.

Mating: Coupling between a male and a female of a species for the purpose of reproducing.

ARMORED INSECTS

Coleoptera (beetles) is the largest order of insects by number of species. Beetles have two sets of wings: The hard, outer wings act as a shell to protect the second, much more delicate pair.

Ladybugs

Ladybugs feed on aphids and other small crop pests. Their color and the number of spots on their shell vary from species to species. When they sense danger, ladybugs secrete a smelly, bad-tasting liquid. Beware to any predator thinking about eating them!

In ancient Egypt, dung beetles were considered sacred insects. To this day, Egyptians wear beetle-shaped jewelry and amulets as good luck charms.

Fireflies

Fireflies emit a characteristic flashing light from a special organ located on their abdomen.

Hercules beetle

One of the biggest insects in the world, the Hercules beetle can grow up to 7 inches long. Only the male has two long, horn-like pincers.

The firefly flashes its light in the dark to attract a mate.

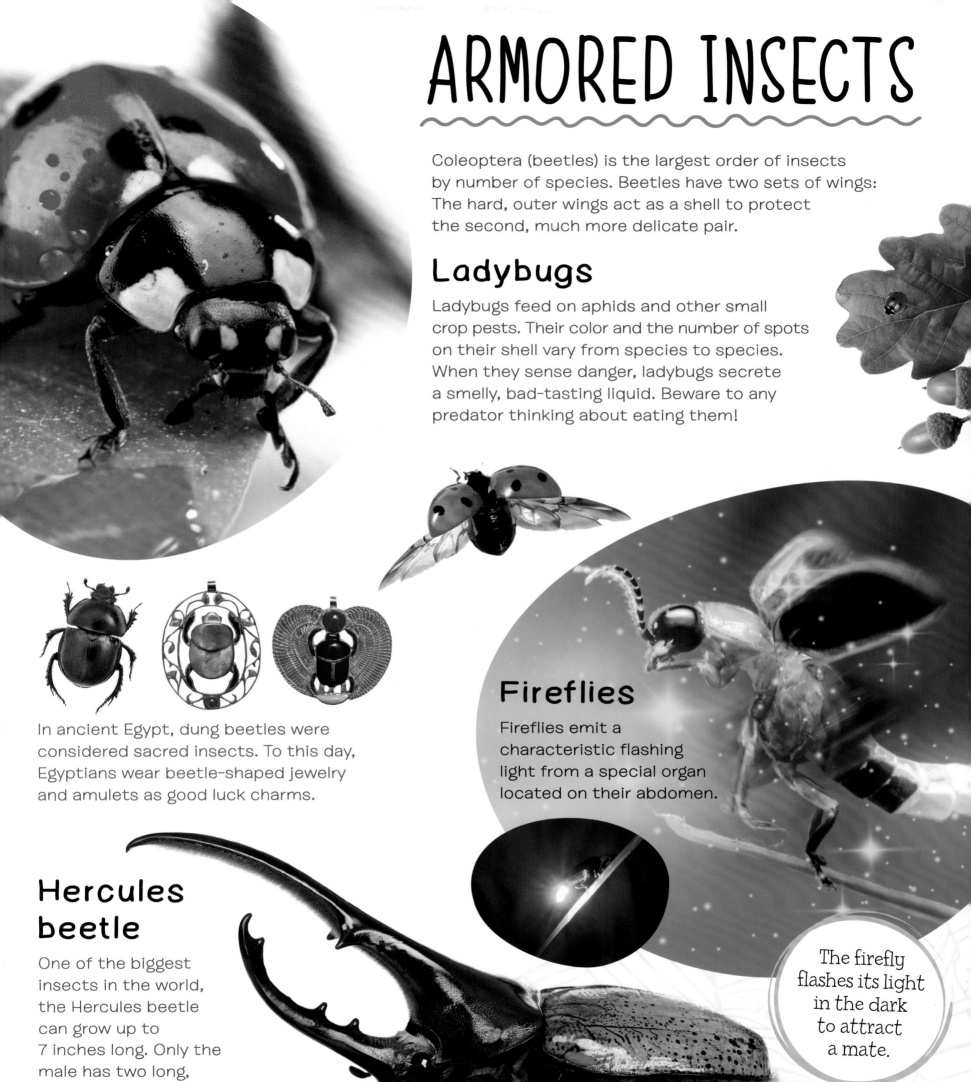

ARACHNIDS

Spiders, scorpions and mites all belong to a class of arthropods called arachnids. Most species in this group are carnivores and produce venom.

Spiders

Spiders have an organ called a spinneret that produces silk. They use this material to spin their web and catch their prey.

Why do spiders spin webs?

Because they can't knit.

Crab spider

Instead of spinning a web, the crab spider adopts a highly ingenious hunting technique: It mimics the behavior of its preferred prey, the ant, to get closer to it.

Mites

Mites are microscopic, meaning they are invisible to the naked eye. They feed on the dead skin cells found in dust. Many people are allergic to them.

Scorpions

Most species of scorpions can be found in the hottest places on Earth. Measuring up to 9 inches long, the emperor scorpion is the largest member of the family.

MYRIAPODS

Myriapods have an articulated body made up of a series of rings. Each of these segments has one or two pairs of legs. They are known familiarly as millipedes!

Julida

Julida have a cylindrical body and roughly 30 pairs of legs. When they sense danger, some species curl up into a spiral to protect themselves.

Scolopendra

Scolopendra are native to the tropics. They have 21 pairs of legs and venomous hooks that can deliver a painful bite to humans.

Scutigera

Scutigera are often found in damp houses. Also called house centipedes, they are not dangerous to humans. Their long back legs look like antennae.

Why was the millipede kicked off his sports team?

Because he took too long to tie his shoes.

MARINE ANIMALS

The world's oceans, seas, lakes and rivers are home to almost one-quarter of all animal species. That's more than 2.2 million species! The seafloors are among the least explored natural environments on the planet, and the farthest reaches of the ocean still hold many mysteries for scientists.

The foundation of the marine ecosystem are phytoplankton, or plant-based plankton, which float on the surface of the world's oceans. Phytoplankton form the base of the aquatic food chain. This type of plankton also produces vast amounts of oxygen—more than 50% of the world's production. Phytoplankton consist of several microscopic species of bacteria and algae.

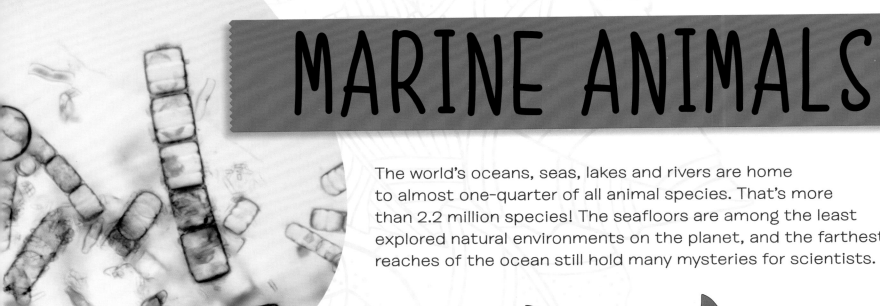

Large predators
(marlins, sharks, etc.)

Fish
(mackerel, tuna, cod, rays, etc.)

Crustacean and fish fry
(juvenile fish)

Zooplankton
(crustaceans, mollusks and fish larvae)

Phytoplankton
(microscopic plants)

What will you find on a cat submarine?

A purriscope

A bathyscaphe is a submersible vehicle designed to explore the ocean depths. Unlike a submarine, which moves horizontally at shallow depths, a bathyscaphe can move vertically and dive very deep under the water.

Biodiversity: All living species and their interactions with each other.

Life underwater

The deeper into lakes, seas and oceans you descend, the less heat and light there are. That's why most marine life is concentrated in the surface layer, in the epipelagic zone.

What is coral?

Polyps are tiny organisms that live in colonies. When free-swimming coral larvae attach themselves to hard surfaces, they turn into polyps and harden. Coral is considered to be a superorganism, because it's comprised of many individuals. Hundreds of coral species exist, and they grow together in large formations called reefs.

Why are coral reefs so important?

Coral reefs have an extremely high level of biodiversity. Many species of fish, crustaceans and mollusks make their homes in the coral reefs. Coral grows very slowly—only a few millimeters per year. Unfortunately, their survival is threatened by environmental factors such as pollution and fishing.

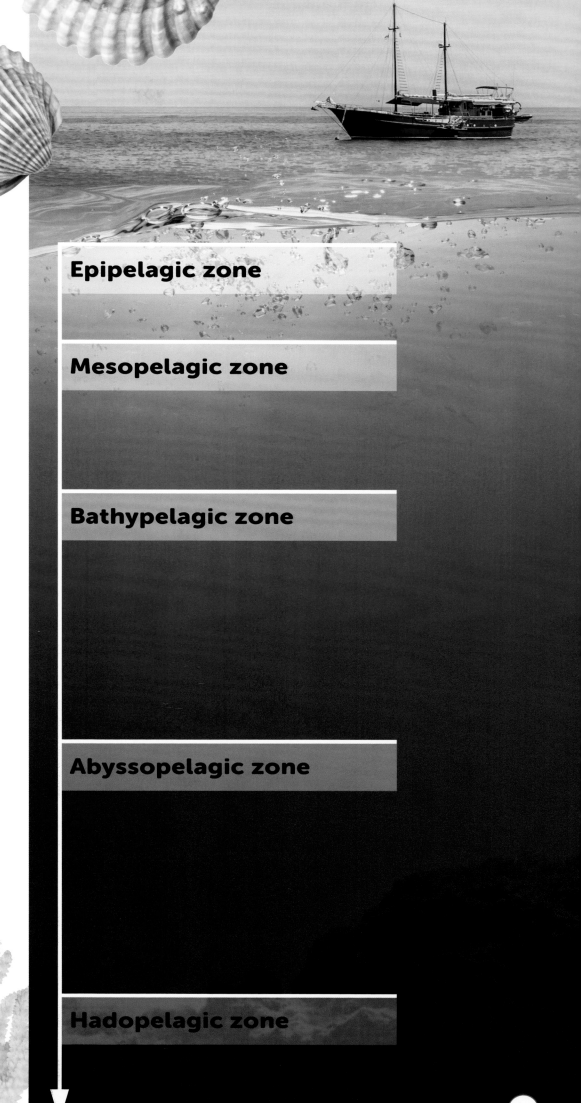

Epipelagic zone

Mesopelagic zone

Bathypelagic zone

Abyssopelagic zone

Hadopelagic zone

FISH

Clownfish

This carnivorous fish, easily recognized by its vibrant colors and white stripes, lives in the tropical oceans. The clownfish lives alone, in a couple, or in a group, in a venomous anemone that protects it from predators.

Class: Fish
Size: 4 inches long
Home: Red Sea, Indian Ocean, Pacific Ocean

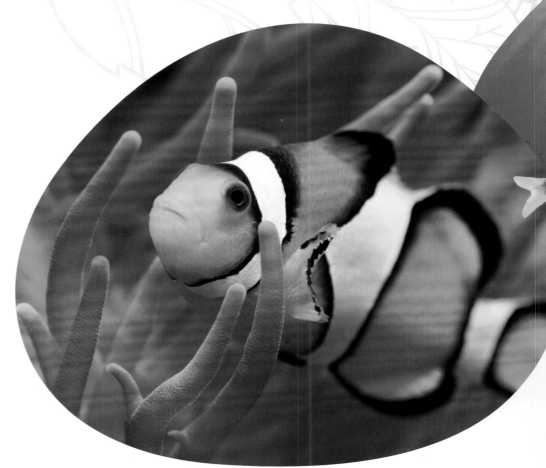

Seahorse

This small, armored fish always swims upright and uses its small dorsal fin to move slowly forward through the water. Seahorses have a very unique way of reproducing. The female deposits her eggs in a pouch on the male's abdomen; he then carries them for three weeks until they hatch.

Class: Fish
Size: .5-14 inches long
Home: Tropical and temperate waters

Barracuda

The great barracuda is a fearsome and opportunistic hunter. The largest of the species can measure up to 6 feet long and swim at top speeds of 25 feet per second. And watch out, because even though they rarely attack humans, barracudas can inflict nasty wounds on reckless divers.

Class: Fish
Size: Up to 6 feet long
Home: Tropical and temperate waters

Cardinal tetra

This small, freshwater fish has brightly colored, metallic scales. The cardinal tetra is a very gregarious species and lives in schools of thousands of individuals; its vast numbers are its only defense mechanism against predators.

Class: Fish
Size: 2 inches long
Home: Rivers and streams of the Amazon rainforest

Flying fish

Flying fish are a family of more than a dozen species with highly developed pectoral fins, which allow them to jump clear out of the water or glide along the surface to escape predators.

Class: Fish
Size: 7-18 inches long
Home: Tropical and temperate waters

Why don't fish play hockey?

Because they're afraid of the net.

Swordfish

This huge predatory fish has a characteristic sword-shaped appendage, called a rostrum, that can measure up to one-third its length. The swordfish is an extremely fast swimmer, reaching top speeds of more than 55 miles per hour.

Class: Fish
Size: 10-14 feet long
Home: Tropical and temperate waters

Gregarious species: Species that live together in groups or organized communities.

OCEAN GIANTS

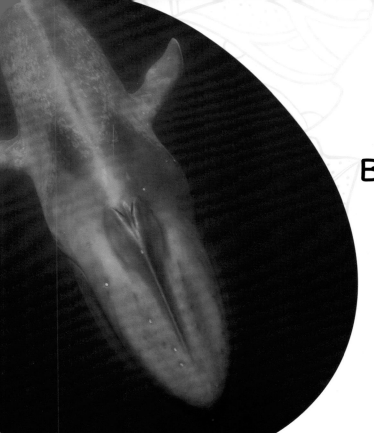

Blue whale

At birth, the biggest animal on Earth already measures 23 feet long! This baleen whale feeds on krill, swallowing up to 4 tons of these tiny crustaceans each day. The global blue whale population is estimated at about 10,000 individuals.

Class: Mammal
Size: 110 feet long
Home: All of the world's oceans, except for the Arctic Ocean

Giant squid

Long considered a mythical creature, the giant squid is a very real species that lives more than one-third of a mile below the surface of the ocean. The squid's mouth, a hard beak that it uses to rip apart its prey, is located at the base of its mantle.

Class: Mollusk / **Size:** 43 feet long / **Home:** Atlantic Ocean

Giant spider crab

The giant spider crab can live to be more than 100 years old. It crawls along the seabed, feeding off animal carcasses and rotting organic matter. The female can lay up to 1.5 million eggs per season, but only a small fraction of them will reach adulthood.

Class: Crustacean
Size: 12 feet long
Home: Pacific Ocean

Echolocation: Location method that consists in sending out calls and receiving the echoes reflected back by various targets to determine their position.

Bottlenose dolphin

The bottlenose dolphin is a highly intelligent, social animal. It communicates with other dolphins in the pod by producing different sounds, whistles and songs. It uses  to find its way around and locate its prey. The female bottlenose dolphin gives birth to one calf every two or three years.

Class: Mammal
Size: 7-9 feet long
Home: Tropical and temperate waters

Dugong

This weird plant-eating marine mammal is nicknamed the "sea cow." Adults can weigh as much as 600 pounds. The dugong spends most of its time foraging for plants that grow on the seabed.

Class: Mammal
Size: 13 feet long
Home: Pacific Ocean and Indian Ocean

Manta ray

At mealtimes, the manta ray opens its mouth wide to swallow huge amounts of water and plankton, which it then filters through its gills. While the manta ray can grow up to 23 feet across and weigh 2 tons, it's actually a gentle, sociable species.

Class: Fish
Size: 15-23 feet across
Home: Tropical and temperate waters

SCARY SHARKS

Whale shark

The whale shark may look intimidating, but it's mostly harmless. Its diet consists of plankton and small fish, which it swallows through its enormous mouth measuring 5 feet across. This fish, the biggest in the world, can filter up to 2,000 tons of water per day for its meals.

Class: Fish
Size: 30-50 feet long
Home: All of the world's oceans

Great white shark

Without a doubt, the great white shark is one of the most fearsome hunters to roam the oceans. This predatory fish feeds on turtles, fish, dolphins and seals, among other animals. It has multiple rows of serrated teeth that grow back when one falls out or breaks.

Class: Fish
Size: 15 feet long
Home: All of the world's oceans

Size: 3 inches

Hammerhead shark

The hammerhead shark's eyes are positioned in a way that allows it to see almost 360°. Along with its eyes, its nostrils, located at either end of its wide head, also give it an edge when hunting. The hammerhead shark is viviparous, meaning the female gives birth to fully formed babies.

Class: Fish
Size: 13 feet
Home: All of the world's oceans

ASTONISHING CREATURES

Anglerfish

Very few species are adapted to life in the deepest reaches of the Earth, where total darkness reigns and food sources are few and far between. However, the anglerfish, which lives at a depth of 6,600 feet, has developed a surprising technique for attracting its prey: The female has a luminous organ that acts like a lure. The light that she produces through bioluminescence attracts small fish, which she then swallows with her enormous mouth.

Sea urchin

The sea urchin's spines, called radioles, act as a form of protection. They're very painful, so this defense mechanism works especially well at intimidating the sea urchin's predators. The bases of the spines are flexible, which also helps the creature to move around. The sea urchin has no eyes and feeds off debris that settles on the ocean floor.

Sea anemone

Although it looks like a plant, the sea anemone is actually an animal that attaches itself to a solid surface, such as a rock, using suction cups. The sea anemone has many venomous tentacles that it uses to capture small prey and bring it to its mouth, which is located in the center of its body.

TEST YOUR KNOWLEDGE!

1. What does the word dinosaur mean?

a) Muscular lizard
b) Terrible lizard
c) Large predator
d) Fossilized bone

2. How big was the largest fossilized dinosaur egg ever found?

a) 50 feet
b) 10 feet
c) 20 inches
d) 1.5 inches

3. What is the ancestor of modern birds?

a) Archaeopteryx
b) Tyrannosaurus
c) Herbivore
d) Brontosaurus

4. What is a person who studies fossils called?

a) Paleontologist
b) Archeologist
c) Arboriculturist
d) Architect

5. What family did Iguanodon belong to?

a) Herbivores
b) Carnivores
c) Iguanas
d) Horned dinosaurs

6. How many vertebrae did Brachiosaurus have in its neck?

a) 24
b) 68
c) 32
d) 12

7. Where is the alpaca native to?

a) South America
b) Europe
c) China
d) Australia

8. How many feathers does a duck have?

a) 50,000
b) 12,000
c) 1,000
d) 58

9. What is different about an ostrich?

a) It eats bread
b) It can't fly
c) It runs slowly
d) It can walk on one foot

10. What does a beaver do when it senses danger?

a) It slaps the water with its tail
b) It eats leaves
c) It dives into the water
d) It runs away

11. Which of these animals is not a reptile?

a) Crocodile
b) Lizard
c) Turtle
d) Butterfly

12. What is the smallest canid in the world?

a) Beaver
b) Weasel
c) Fennec fox
d) Grey wolf